One Hundred and Forty-Two Thoughts Of a Convicted Felon

One Hundred and Forty-Two Thoughts of a Convicted Felon is dedicated to those who seek a better understanding of the criminal thinking process. It is also dedicated to the chosen few people that supported and had faith in us, when we didn't have it in ourselves.

Table of Contents

1. "The Plan"
2. "My Life (Part One)"
3. "My Everyday Schedule"
4. "Followers"
5. "The Guide"
6. "Advice"
7. "Out of Sight, Out of Mind"
8. "Past and Present"
9. "Consequences"
10. "They Love That (Part One)"
11. "#1 Excuse"
12. "Misery Loves Company"
13. "Real Estate"
14. "Fallen Soldier"
15. "What Should I Do?"
16. "We"
17. "Day Dreams"
18. "Family"
19. "Past Actions"
20. "Correspondence (Part One)"
21. "Broken Promises"
22. "Façade?"
23. "Flip Side"
24. "Choices"
25. "Cohabitation"
26. "Materialistic"
27. "America's Nightmare"
28. "Alias"
29. "Marathon"
30. "Role Model"
31. "Whorehouse"
32. "Trial"
33. "Farewell"
34. "The Game"
35. "Everyday"
36. "Before"
37. "After"
38. "Hindsight"
39. "Love"
40. "Side Streets"
41. "Idiot Box (Part One)"
42. "The Corner"

43. "Day & Night"
44. "Freedom"
45. "Correspondence (Part Two)"
46. "Ear Crack"

47. "Trees"
48. "Cognizant"
49. "Why?"
50. "Illusion"
51. "Life's Exam"
52. "Neutral"
53. "Survival"
54. "Smoke"
55. "Thoroughfare"
56. "Twenty Questions"
57. "Palter"
58. "Her"
59. "Karma"
60. "Time's Curse"
61. "Never"
62. "Mistakes"
63. "Wildflowers"
64. "Words of Wisdom"
65. "Remember"
66. "Loses"
67. "Faith"
68. "My Life (Part Two)"
69. "It"
70. "6 Minutes"
71. "The Crime"
72. "The Trial"
73. "The Verdict"
74. "Stop"
75. "Unconditionally"
76. "Correspondence (Part 3)"
77. "Rain Drops"
78. "Substance"
79. "Fanciful Escape"
80. "Self-Service"
81. "Improvise"
82. "Waves of Romance"
83. "Institutionalized"
84. "Nether World"
85. "Trust Issues"
86. "Idiot Box (Part Two)"
87. "Synthesis"
88. "Passionate Attachment"
89. "Real Differences"
90. "M.A.Y.A.N.T.S."
91. "You"

92. "Routine"
93. "The Root of All Evil"
94. "Issues"

95. "Differently"
96. "Optical Illusion"
97. "Pretty Brown Eyes"
98. "Correspondence (Part Four)"
99. "Concrete Jungle"
100. "Face to Face"
101. "Culpable"
102. They Love That (Part Two)"
103. "They Love That (Part Two)"
104. "Workout"
105. "Approximately"
106. "Daddy's Little Girl"
107. "The Last Place"
108. "Purgatory"
109. "Evolution"
110. "Contemplation"
111. "Last Walk"
112. "Never Too Late"
113. "Addict"
114. "Correspondence (Part Five)"
115. "Slick Talk"
116. "S.I.N.F.U.L."
117. "Quid Pro Quo"
118. "Touch It"
119. "Communication"
120. "Correspondence (Part Six)"
121. "Lost in Thought"
122. "Pink Slip"
123. "Vindictive"
124. "Tell Me"
125. "War"
126. "Currency"
127. "Excuses"
128. "The Theory"
129. "Eyes Wide Shut"
130. "My Life (Part Three)"
131. "Unbecoming"
132. "Beautiful"
133. "Correspondence (Part Seven)"
134. "Years Later"
135. "They Love That (Part Three)"
136. "Only"
137. "Great Oak"
138. "My Auntie"
139. "Your Day"

140. "Interchangeable"
141. "Greatest Fear"
142. "My Only Regret"

"The Plan"

I use the past as a blueprint,
    of things that I shouldn't do.

Because things that I used to do,
    were considered against the rules.

The things that I shouldn't do,
    got my family missing me too.

Because things I used to do,
    got me sentenced one-forty-two.

"My Life (Part One)"

When I passed through the gates, I left the block behind. Cars, clothes, fancy broads, and even the hop behind. I never thought I'd see a place where they could stop my grind. Locked down 22 hours in a box confined. A lot of time just to think, plan, and plot my crimes. To make sure no more associates can drop a dime. The out of sight and out of mind clouds have blocked my shine. The same broads that stopped the ride, won't even drop a line. And my partners that claimed to ride or die, just rise and fly. Baby mothers have lied and lied about sliding by. But I ain't mad, I keep my head up and eyes on the prize. They want to see the signs, the judge laughed when he gave me this time. I asked him "How am I supposed to do it?" "Day by day" he replied. And since they sent me off to prison, Ken and my Grandfather died. Along with Smoke and Mike G, who lost their lives over highs. But the thought of losing them, can't even bring me to cry. Because I'm too caught up in my pride, to let them fall from demise. When the only reason they are still alive, is because I let them survive. Plus, I watched street crews divide, over homosexual ties. Because one is sexing a guy, and the other's questioning why.

"My Everyday Schedule"

```
5:00AM    Breakfast
7:00AM    Custody Count
10:00AM   Lunch
12:00PM   Custody Count
3:00PM    Custody Count
4:00PM    Dinner
5:15PM    Custody Count
8:15PM    Custody Count
11:00PM   Custody Count
```

    I have been told that the definition of insanity is doing the same thing over and over again looking for a different outcome.
        After 9 years of this, am I insane?

"Followers"

Unconscious are those lost souls born to follow another's cause.

Motivated only by the pursuit of their leader's happiness.

Lacking the testicular fortitude to choose their own path.

While giving all of themselves to a cause that will not benefit them in any type of way.

Blessed is the man that controls an army of followers, because he will never be put in harms way.

But cursed is the army of followers, because their personal sacrifices will be looked over at the end of the day.

"The Guide"

I suffer the consequences of my actions, looking forward only to another day in the same rotation.

To complain would be a waste of energy, so I am forced to find other ways to vent my frustrations.

Motivated only by the thoughts of what could, should, and probably will be.

Waiting patiently for my turn to come before the powers that be, praying this time around I will get free.

Unable to forgive or forget the calendars that I will never get back, all because of the words of another.

While hoping that my trials and tribulations become a guide for those behind me, so they never have to endure my stress and struggle.

"Advice"

How can I not admit that everything that I have, had, or will ever receive, did not come from my mother?

She is my creator, and I bow before her to ask for her blessings for whatever righteous or unrighteous endeavor I may pursue.

Unconscious of the effect she has had over my existence, I move forward unconcerned with the consequences of my actions.

Blessed with her words of wisdom, her motherly advice does not make sense until after I fail at my task.

Sorry cannot begin to make up for my stupidity, so I ask that you allow me the opportunity to begin the healing process with a sincere apology.

Please forgive me for my ignorance, but I needed to endure this torture, so I could completely understand how much your advice means to me.

"Out of Sight, Out of Mind"

While the opportunity presented itself to smile, laugh, and engage in useless conversations,

I was a constant thought in the minds of those that saw me on a regular basis.

Following the code of the streets,

I made my presence known to those that looked to me in their times of need.

Putting all my extra energy aside to give to those that claimed to love me.

I knew that my lifestyle came with repercussions that would clarify who actually begrudged me.

As the sands of time traveled through the hourglass of life, mistakes were made that completely changed my existence,

And after years of moving fast against the grain, I became a part of the system…

At that point the smiles, laughs, and useless conversations that were routine,

Changed to smirks, frowns, and conversations that were few and far between.

Staying true to the unwritten laws of the avenues,

I reached out to collect on debts that were well overdue.

In my times of need, I searched for the positive energy to move me.

So as the days, weeks, months, and years slowly passed me by,

It became clear to me, that the consequences of my actions, had made me truly…

Out of Sight, and Out of Mind!

"Past and Present"

How is it that this country was discovered, when countless tribes of Indians already inhabited the land?

Lies and deception were the building blocks for their takeover, and present-day Slave Masters still follow the old habits of their clan.

Taken from our homeland to serve as slaves, because bosses didn't feel the need to do any work.

Their wealth was only as good as their help, and broken spirits push and pull without conscious until it hurts.

Spreading their wings, they covered the whole country in search of fresh ground to claim as their own.

Destroying anything that interfered with their progress, and 500 years later the same thing still goes on.

Now the titles have been changed, but the work is still being done inside of their Correctional Facilities.

With judges controlling the slave trade, after convictions give them the right to take away everything including a man's liberties.

The whips and chains have been traded in for pens and pieces of paper.

That make even the strongest men follow unusual rules and regulations.

Those that follow a path other than the straight and narrow, gives the new Slave Masters the opportunity to add them to their plantations.

And just like centuries before, freedom becomes a memory and part of everyday conversation.

"Consequences"

As one under privileged individual made decisions that would change his life in the worst way, the repercussions of his actions were a thought lost in the back of his mind,

The situation in front of him that contained poverty and possibilities, truly motivated of an environment that rewarded the strong and punished the weak,

He fell victim to the pressures of self preservation, and lived each moment as if it were his last, with something to prove.

Lacking the skills to do anything other than hustle, he made the conscious decision to survive in the ways of those that he watched.

Taking time to do his research, he jumped into the pharmaceutical trade following the rules and regulations that he had picked up from conversations with those that were living well.

Applying his second-hand information with the knowledge that was blessed to him, he became one of the many salesmen that pushed product to those that were willing to do anything for it.

Avoiding the normal routine of the corner salesman, he learned from the mistakes of his peers, and advanced his business from retail to wholesale.

Planning to leave the lifestyle that supported his entire organization when he achieved the goal that he had set for himself,

He found himself unable to walk away from the game, when his financial situation reached that number.

But just like those before him, unforeseeable circumstances opened his eyes to a situation that was out of his control.

And before he was able to somewhat rectify the problem, he was arrested, processed, and given the opportunity to witness his employees take him under.

"They Love That (Part One)"

Diabolical the plan, plotted, schemed, and measured. Taking us for granted, and they wonder why we are scandalous. It's hard enough to understand life itself. Just watching my every step, only controlling my breaths. Please forgive me, they got me demented, wrapped in the system. Like presents for Christmas, got me unconsciously wishing. That I could be forgiven, for every sin a lavish living. It's hard to deal with it, be real with it, and know it. Didn't grow up with a father, so momma made me a soldier. Only kept my composure, through drinking and blowing dosa. Running from the rollers, and watching out for the cobras. Poisonous venom from the streets, and I still feel it. Convicted felon chilling, my momma made me a realist.

Who love that?

"#1 Excuse"

When complaints turn to conversations about a solution to the problem,

Most use a crutch to keep from personally addressing the issue.

Not wanting to be the first to act against what they feel is an injustice to them,

They use other's previous failures as their reason for not being a leader.

Confident that their actions will not be followed up by those around them,

They choose to point the finger instead of making a contribution because they fear retaliation.

The pen has been proclaimed to be more dangerous than the sword,

But no one uses the same tactics because written complaints about cruel and unusual punishment get swept under the rug.

Changes cannot be made in one day,

But the baby steps that will bring about the same results are never spoken about.

"Ain't nobody gonna ride,"

Is the most common thing said when questioning a complainer about the reason why he won't personally stand up for himself.

"Misery Loves Company"

Meaningful moments make memories that motivate man, when miserable miscalculations manipulate his ability to maneuver.

Ignorant to the ideas influenced by incarceration, individuals imagine intimate illusions immune to the insanities integrated inside of the institution.

As aggression and agitation alters ambitions, angry atmospheres and adversities that antagonize all associated with asinine authority.

Correctional Centers consciously cause convicts to continue criminal cultivation, by concentrating on complete confinement for calendars.

Purposely putting people in pitiful positions, praying that their penitentiaries properly promote premeditated passive punishment.

Unable to understand their ultimate goal, men unconsciously utilize crime to uplift the underdog.

While warriors already within the walls, welcome anyone without wisdom willing to walk the path of the worthless weekly.

"Real Estate"

Why would he work, when the tuft has supported him in his times of need? Dedicated to the same street, that he lived on all his life. The same block that introduced him to rocks, the throwing and smoking kind. Not blind to his surroundings, he watched any and everything around him. Because when he felt lost, the block found him, and showed him the love that he longed for. Ready to die for his homeboys, he went through the courting process and became a member of his street's gang. Given a new name, he did everything within his power to live up to it. Following the code of his street, he started beef with anybody from rival blocks. Colors became his friends and foes, because they let him know who was who. Staying true was all that mattered, so he lived by the words "death before dishonor." Not even his momma could stop him from claiming his block until opposition made him a casualty of war. Even though liquor was poured, nothing could change the fact that he was gone. Not even grown, he died for a piece of land that nobody in his gang owned.

"Fallen Soldier"

Miserable is the soldier that has fallen from grace, and been reduced to a government name and number. Taken under by the rapture of fast money, women, and the lifestyle that he witnessed from the side line as he waited patiently for his chance to get in the game. Blamed for any and everything that didn't go according to plan. He played his hand to the best of his ability, not concerned with what could have been. Life was his gift and curse, so he flirted with death hoping that it would take him away from the sad routine that he lived from day to day. Crime become his mistress, while misfits did everything in their power to please him. Pistols gave him everything that he ever wanted, so he continued to take any and everything that caught his attention. Addicted to being unrestricted by the street code, he paid no mind to the laws of the avenues. His attitude showed nothing but arrogance, because he didn't respect anything. But inside of his dreams, all that he had seen in the past that he truly feared. And unclear of what it actually meant, he bent with the thought of life in jail, he rebelled and showed the world exactly what it expected from him. After being processed, he took countless conquests, because he refused to surrender. Leaving behind his nickname, he accepted the title of offender. A true beginner to the prison scene, his silent screams tell the real story of what his life means.

"What Should I Do?"

I am nothing to me,
    I am something to you.
I am without a clue,
    asking what should I do?
With You,
    I am in between a rock and where I want to be.
Confused,
    because I know exactly what I want for me.
Love, happiness,
    and a person to share my feelings.
Emotional ups and downs,
    on this roller coaster of living,
Good, bad,
    and all the above.
Blended with just enough love,
    to make sure that every moment is a plus.
But I have been hurt before,
    in ways that I will never forget.
To the extent,
    that the past controls my present events.
And that's thicker than blood,
    So much that I am only left with a grudge
Against anything close,
    to like, lust, or love!
That is the main reason,
    I am indifferent towards any type of commitment,
Because I know without a doubt,
    with love comes consequences.
And my present situation,
    makes it harder for me to face it.
Incarcerated,
    expressing my deepest feelings on paper.
Praying,
    that you can comprehend half of what I've written.
Because half,
    is more than enough to tell you how I am feeling.
Truthfully,
    I am more than confused.
Because even when the sun's up it's dark,
    I have nothing to lose.
Put yourself in my position,
    and think about it for a minute.
Who would benefit,
    honestly from beginning to ending?
And I know,
    that being alone is rough.
But all I can give you from jail is love
    and love won't be enough…

"We"

While following in the footsteps of those that set the standard, we took advantage of every negative opportunity that presented itself. Influenced by the pursuit of wealth, we dealt drugs to anyone financially able to afford the products that we sold. We set goals that were ten times what we expected to receive. Our greed for material things, made spending money second on our list of priorities because the game was built on competition. Unafraid of the consequences, we sold illegal pieces of hope while watching for the police, and endured nights of no sleep, because customers came until the sun came up with balled up money in their hands. Making supply and demand a logical excuse for our actions. Finding no satisfaction in our occupation, we concentrated on self-medication to numb our senses. Truly addicted to the drug trade and all the money that we made, we played the game unaware of the repercussions. We held discussions about other illegal activities, while passing stuffed cigars, for our own personal gain. We sold cocaine, because we watched our role models do the same. Blamed for being a part of the problem instead of the solution, we continued to keep moving because we had nothing to lose. Lost and confused, we sold our product to friends and family members that used because we knew, if not us, then who?

"Day Dreams"

As convicts reminisce about their past life, they glorify all the moments that contributed to their incarceration. Fascinated with the criminal lifestyle, their stories give explicit descriptions of situations they experienced. Proud of their conversations they never speak of rehabilitation. Their topics usually consist of violent altercations, drug related cases, or women with ample breast, apple bottoms, and pretty faces. Depressed by their memories that they use for motivation. Completely separated from family and friends, thoughts of revenge become premeditated plans to commit sins. Lacking the ability to express themselves with words, their actions show how disturbed they have become during their time behind the fences. Cursed with felony convictions, their day dreams become contradictions of what could have been. Stress becomes a constant reminder of what should have been, while reality adds insult to injury. Used to the misery, most convicts wonder if their fate was meant to be, as they day dream about the next time they will get to see the streets.

"Family"

      The same flesh and blood that never lies to me, has the same pride as me, and supports me in my times of need. Those that love me unconditionally, whether day or night, wrong or right, positive or negative. They are my relatives, and can relate to my stress and strain. Able to feel my pain, because we share the same blood, color, and name. My family tree's branches spread from sea to sea, seed to seed, and those in need receive assistance. Generations dedicated to that commitment. Fathers, Mothers, Sisters, Brothers, Aunts, Uncles, and Cousins all connected. All respected, because they come when they are called in planes, trains, and cars. Ready to get involved in any problem that needs to be solved whether financial or physical. They are the miracle, and their movements are memorable. Proud to be a part of that, with them is where the heart is at, and that makes us complete. Love without competition, love without consequences, and most of all love without contradictions. From young to old, all with the same goal of keeping family first, is the only way we make it work.

"Past Actions"

While being loyal to those that we loved, instead of those that loved us, bridges were burnt down.

Connections were disconnected, because people involved didn't receive the same love they gave out quid pro quo.

Simple conversations escalated to extreme arguments, and gentle gestures were interpreted in the wrong ways.

Compliments were taken as insults, because the distance between all parties involved couldn't be overcome.

Decisions about resolutions were made without thinking, because angry emotions turned assumptions into facts.

Calendars contributed to changes that were unseen, and personal growth was ignored because grudges were established.

The thin line between love and hate was crossed constantly, because a mutual understanding could not be achieved.

Lacking the ability to put the past aside, each step forward was followed by two steps in the opposite direction.

"Correspondence (Part One)"

Dear Self,

Ello Hapy Irty day, how is life treating you? Very well I pray, even though we don't talk like we used to do. As for myself, you already know this prison shit is complicated. But I can sum it up in 7 words- I'm just here and I hate it! Besides that, there really ain't nothing more I can say. It's the same ole bullshit here, just another day.

Enough about my situation, how is the family and all of them bitches? Since I ain't seen you in a minute, if you got some shoot me some pictures. I know you probably wondering when I'm gonna get released. But the truth is, I can't say when I'm gonna touch the streets. You know how these people play it, and what this shit is all about. It's easy to get locked up, but hard as fuck to get out!

I just pray that you don't follow in my footsteps little brother. This some real game uddy cay, please don't let it go in one ear and right out of the other. Life in the fast lane ain't worth the consequences. I would prefer to be broke and disgusted then stuck inside of these fences.

But if you choose to hustle, be careful because the game is twisted. Remember that I am here because niggas be snitching. The streets are full of animals, so try your best to avoid the cobras. And the most important thing is to keep your friends close and your enemies closer.

With that out of the way, I will let you go for now. But I need you to know that I love you, so hold me down. Also let your family know that I will love them until the day that I die. So until we speak again, keep your head up and eyes on the prize.

Quid pro quo,
Gee'z

P.S.

Be easy!

"Broken Promises"

Believing those words,
Relieved that they were heard.
Obligations made with passionate intentions,
Knowing the consequences of that commitment.
Emotional connections were created.
Negotiations were premeditated.

Procrastination became a part of your personality,
Responsibility became its first casualty.
Oaths lost their validity,
Mutual understanding became a memory.
Illusions showed me what you wanted me to see,
Silence granted me unabridged reality.
Educated to life's faulty notions,
Standard agreements are made to be broken.

"Façade"

Stuck between a rock and a hard place, the hard way seems to be the only way out, when the only way out is in.

Those on the outside looking in will only see a reflection, because most illusions are based on the deception of perception.

We only see what we want to see, because tunnel vision's contradictions don't allow complete comprehension of everything that we have witnessed.

Opinions assume the role of facts, while appearances become victims of prejudice before intelligence or relevance can be determined.

Information is broken down into molecules, and modern views are misinterpreted by every hue, because they refuse to pay attention.

Unwilling to come to any type of compromise, unconscious minds choose to label what they see by color and creed, and agree to disagree.

"Flip Side"

With love comes hate,
With smiles come frowns.
With achievements come failures,
With ups come downs.
With positives come negatives,
With happiness comes agitation.
With knowledge comes ignorance,
With unity comes separation.
With questions come answers,
With problems come solutions.
With blessings come curses,
With clarity comes confusion.
With addition comes subtraction,
With right comes left.
With pleasure comes pain,
With life comes death.

"Choices"

Missing the things left behind because the crime came with Consequences. Those stuck behind the fences either search for repentance or hone their criminal senses. Sentenced to years inside of the system, where trust and commitment are almost nonexistent, even the straightest thoughts become tangled and twisted. Hunters continue to take victims, whereas the others take to religion hoping that biblical scriptures can prolong their existence, while those indifferent to religious assistance continue on the path of least resistance. Unconcerned with spiritual forgiveness those that resist it put revenge on their wish list, and take avarice as a sixth sense. Crime becomes their mistress, while their counterparts' persistence is looked at like bitch shit, because given the choice between with it or against it their ignorance is consistent.

"Cohabitation"

Never ending conversations filled with
complaints and observations, cause
personal frustrations that cannot be
compensated over long durations.

Different personalities that interpret
reality from different perspectives,
are coerced into finding that one
connection that has a suitable reflection.

Trapped inside of a small place where
personal space is often a high commodity,
civil comradery becomes an oddity
throughout the prison odyssey.

Forced to coexist with individuals whose
personal rituals whether devilish or
spiritual, contribute to making
incarceration more miserable.

Those new to this experience, become
willing participants in an experiment
to see which personalities can truly
coexist inside a cell behind the fence.

"Materialistic"

Preoccupied with the accumulation of dead presidents, precious metals, stones, and elements, all other righteous endeavors become irrelevant.

Following the so-called trends, set by athletes, rappers, and friends, many women and men waste all their ends in a sad attempt to fit in.

Infatuated with personal possessions, the collection of material times becomes an obsession, that combats all forms of rejection.

Blinded by greed, the dedication, determination, and discipline to succeed, becomes less important than wants, but more important than needs.

"America's Nightmare"

America's nightmare is not terrorism.

It has nothing to do with hostages, plane hijackings, suicide
bombers, or racism because those situations can be avoided.

America's nightmare is not STDs.

It has nothing to do with gonorrhea, genital herpes, hepatitis,
or HIV, because those types of infection can be prevented.

America's nightmare is not crime.

It has nothing to do with burglary, robbery, assault, or murder,
because those offenses can be punished.

America's nightmare is not narcotics.

It has nothing to do with marijuana, cocaine, heroin, or
methamphetamines, because those addictions can be treated.

America's nightmare is not gangs.

It has nothing to do with Crips, Bloods, Disciples, or
Vice Lords, because those organizations can be controlled.

America's nightmare is education.

It has everything to do with knowledge, wisdom, understanding,
and experience, because those qualities dominate out society.

"Alias"

The most important thing to me isn't myself,
it's my creator.

The essence and aura of the being that made
my existence possible.

The one that sacrificed her wants, to make
sure that I had everything that I needed.

The individual responsible for my over
confidence.

The woman that taught me everything that
I know.

The strongest person I have ever seen in
my life.

She has many titles and nicknames, but only
one is important to me.

She was, is, and always will be, the one
I call Momma!

"Marathon"

After many moments of intimate passion, climax's fireworks signal the start of the race.

Thousands of willing participants vie for position, as they travel through nature's obstacle course.

Only the strongest contender will cross the finish line, so all competitors give their all, because second place is not an option.

Those not strong enough to accomplish their goal fall to the wayside, while those endowed With knowledge and strength continue moving forward.

After enduring all of the trials and tribulations that come with their journey, only a chosen few make it to the last stage of the race.

And as the finish line rapidly approaches, rules and regulations become irrelevant as self-preservation takes over.

Friendly competition escalates to fierce rivalry, as all parties involved fight for possession of the trophy.

Knowing that there can only be one winner, the competitor that gains entry into the winner's circle, ensures that all other participants involved in that race will not achieve their ultimate potential.

"Role Model"

Raised in an environment where violence and understanding go hand in hand, role models are not chosen because of their positive contributions to society.

Many young black males tend to follow in the footsteps of criminals, drug addicts, and gang members, because those are the only people they see on a regular basis.

Adolescents unable to overcome poverty, set aside their knowledge of right and wrong to follow the bad influences that have acquired what they truly desire.

Parents unwilling to be positive role models, unconsciously give their children the chance to fall victim to the street life.

Communities tired of trying to combat the problem, concede defeat without putting forth any type of positive effort to save the uncorrupted.

Making consequences and repercussions truly irrelevant, because self-preservation is the ultimate kind of motivation in any and every type of situation.

"Whorehouse"

Placed in a compromising position, where the difference between freedom and captivity depends on snitching, many become witnesses for the prosecutor. And just like sexual prostitution, deceit and confusion is used to acquire the best potential. Labeled as confidential, their new whores secret conversations become monumental pieces of information, used in the investigation. Unscrupulous individuals willing to engage in intimate oral exchanges for judicial arrangements previous to arraignment, are the new prostitutes. Those that have long promiscuous verbal relations to avoid incarceration, are the reasons that countless crooks catch unreported cases. Written statements and taped confessions taken from the whores in question, teach valuable lessons to new tricks involved in criminal indiscretions.

"Trial"

In a fair trial, a jury of my peers would
consist of a Murderer, Gambler, Drug Addict,
Hood Rat, Armed Robber, Pharmaceutical Dealer,
Exotic Dancer, Cat Burglar, Car Thief,
Alcoholic, Gold Digger, and a Gang Member,
because our occupations are somewhat equal.

But instead of my peers, I received a jury
of their peers, that consisted of a Doctor,
Stock Broker, Therapist, Housewife,
Security Guard, Catholic Preacher,
Soccer Mom, Construction Worker, Bartender,
Car Salesman, Store Owner, and a Teacher,
because my peers are not considered people.

"Farewell"

As we travel in our separate ways,

moving at our separate pace,

hopefully our paths will never cross again.

We were not meant to be,

so as you walk away from me,

hopefully we will never talk again.

No more angry conversations,

Or heated altercations,

Because there is no more us.

No need to waste your lies,

on second tries,

because there is no more trust.

Was lust the cause,

behind it all,

or just a small piece?

That hurt my soul,

then changed my goals,

and made me leave the streets.

The Game

It started with strict rules and regulations,
but after more people placed applications
to get involved in the occupation, its
compensation quickly escalated to constant
hatred.

Crack's creation caused further separation
between the races, because it was not a
poor problem in its beginning stages.

But with time comes changes, and normal
routines ran into complications, when the
game allowed anyone to set up illegal
formations to accumulate paper.

That situation caused countless confrontations,
because personal frustrations interfered
with concentration on money making.

At that point, the game became a competition,
where family and friends became opposition,
because with money came dire consequences.

Comrades and enemies switched positions,
And anyone manipulated by their pursuit
of riches never seen the top position,
because the game's mission was to ruin
everyone it caught with the get rich
quick proposition.

"Everyday"

People are given the choice to choose
between right and wrong, but as life goes
on it becomes harder to right our wrongs,
because they accumulate.

Really each injustice deserves separate
repentance, but life's consequences
don't allow enough time to address
individual issues.

Anyone able to spare a moment of precious
time can give a silent confession, to
apologize for their multiple indiscretions,
and express gratitude for their blessings.

Yesterday's movements are the past whether
righteous or unrighteous, with or without
a purpose, above or below the surface,
those moments of prayer are worth it.

"Before"

Before ramifications became his compensation, his occupation consisted of a combination of manipulation and intimidation. His pigmentation added complications to his situation like discrimination, misrepresentation, and financial separation, but those frustrations were normal accommodations inside of his civilization. Lacking the proper education, sophistication, and qualifications to apply for a position in administration, his aggravation, irritation, agitation, indignation, and desperation was his concentration, consultation, and calculation. He acquired the information needed to gain real emancipation. The temptation to take reparations from organizations without negotiations or explanations was reciprocation for segregation's domination. Unable to follow rules and regulations, his visual presentations were demonstrations of controlled hatred. His operation used cooperation, communication, and conversations to help with its accumulation of dead denominations. Until several miscalculations, confrontations, and identifications led to the deterioration of his criminal formation.

"After"

After months of investigations, observations, speculations, and careful considerations, the extermination of his fortification became a realization. Interrogations done without representation on members of his organization, led to criminal litigations and incarceration when dedication didn't live up to its expectations. Insinuations, implications, fabrications, and resignations were the culmination before the jury's deliberation. Knowing their obligation to his city's legislation, his guesstimation of his stipulations didn't have limitations. His imagination said probation, while the jury gave its recommendation for a long duration of isolation. Thinking of ways to get retaliation, the thoughts of suffocation, strangulation, controlled starvation, extreme anal violation, and cremation all crossed his mind while the judge made a declaration for a continuation of his trial and tribulations. Seeking salvation, he used illegal medications for stimulation until that sensation produced a hallucination/revelation of criminal hibernation inside of a rehabilitation plantation.

"Hindsight"

Given the opportunity to go back to past
moments, different choices can be made to
avoid the mistakes that have changed our
existence.

Misconceptions could be clarified, to get
a better understanding of confusing
situations.

Misunderstanding could be resolved without
arguments and confrontations, because the
truth is available.

Unhealthy relationships could be avoided
or terminated, before they start to become
a problem.

Bad decisions could be eliminated or
rectified, because their result is
already known.

Addictions could be prevented or controlled,
and experiences whether good or bad could
be handled accordingly.

But the past is only the past because its
moments cannot be changed and getting
the chance to revisit past events would
ruin the meaning of life, because experience
is the best teacher, and changing the past
would alter the future.

"Love"

Samples of this substance can have dangerous
repercussions, because even one use has
been known to cause addiction.

Extreme pleasure or unexplainable pain can
be received from watered down versions of
the product, and its narcotic substitutes
are just as addictive.

Consumption can be achieved by several
different methods, but once inside of the
system, the effects are usually the same.

The product is normally taken in small doses,
because over exposure can cause dependency
quicker than any other medication.

Abuse is common, and addiction to the product
has severe consequences because no amount
of money can purchase real love.

"Side Streets"

Conversations based on part truth and part lies may be more interesting than the boring facts, but they also send mixed messages that can be misinterpreted or taken the wrong way. At the crossroads where Truth and Lies intersect, the corners hold clues to the real identity of the person you are dealing with. So when searching for answers that truly make sense, a trip must be made to the corner of Truth and Lies where Knowledge, Ignorance, Confidence, and Insecurity are located, because personal image is only an optical illusion that can be clearly seen, if it is looked at from the right side of the street.

"Idiot Box (Part One)"

When the Real World is not the Most Extreme, the Young and the Restless turn to Mad TV for an Intervention. Not wanting to be the Weakest Link, those that have One Life to Live usually start Wild'N Out, because they don't want to get Punk'd. So As the World Turns, All My Children that represent Rap City and South Park live by the code of Dog Eat Dog, because Law & Order is an Unsolved Mystery. Master Minds know that It Takes a Thief to live like an American Idol, but Friends of the People's Court put all that in serious Jeopardy, because they will help the Cops shut down the Cash Cab by telling them Whose Line it is. Then the Girl Friend Who Wants to be a Millionaire loses her Love Connection and takes you to Divorce Court, because the King of the Hill that Pimp My Ride, Trick My Truck, and sold you that American Chopper is ready to be her Family Guy. And that may cause a Family Feud for 60 Minutes, but after the First 48 the Wife Swap will either be a Deal or No Deal, because The Apprentice will learn that his new Moesha has Grey's Anatomy and very bad Lingo. And even though the Monster House might seem like the Animal Precinct for the first 24 because Drew Carey tells you What Not to Wear, and Dr. 90210 needs to go back to College Hill, after you see the Cold Case Files, it will have a Direct Effect on your thoughts about Prison Break. So while you think about Soul Food and Sex and the City, the Days of Our Lives inside of The Center are a Comic View of True Life in one of America's Funniest Home Videos.

"The Corner"

Following the domino's as they fell, being broke seemed to be the closest thing to hell, while we enjoyed heaven on Earth. Wanting everything first, we looked at work as a simple waste of time. From 9 to 5, just to survive, while corners made more. The things we saved for, they already bought and paid for, with money to spare. The money was there and always was, because drugs got peddled there years before us. By the same O.G.'s that showed us how to rock up the gold dust, and where it came from. The same O.G.'s that we got our game from, and most of our names from, but that was only the start. To play the corner was an art, that took part smarts and part heart, to make the money. Good product would keep the friends coming, skipping and humming, with something when the paper ran out. Not looking for a hand out, they would fan out, and find things to trade for it. Steal things to pay for it, and when all else failed, they would even sell themselves unable to control their addiction. Its consequences caused emotional contradictions, because the rush was all that mattered. Users and dealers both with habits, and the corner helped its addicts, because only the faces changed. Used to the stress and strain of the game, the corner stayed the same, while its victims changed.

"Day & Night"

With anger and depression being the constant
emotional state of offenders and convicts,
hatred and frustration ae common excuses
used to justify ignorant and violent behavior.

Rules and regulations set up to ruin even
the smallest piece of hope, are changed
depending on the situation and circumstances
to whatever benefits the institution.

Compensation and restitution paid to society
for mistakes and miscalculations, are the
only consequences and repercussions that come
with crime and punishment.

While state and local government continue
to invent new laws and stipulations, promoting
revenge and retaliation instead of reform
and rehabilitation.

"Freedom"

When the only way to deal with reality
is by not thinking about it, our
imaginations form an alternate reality that
is easier to live with. Unable to deal
with our present situations mentally,
the mind uses memories to paint a
pleasant picture. More fiction than
reality usually, vivid images of how
it used to be mixed with delusions of
grandeur. Lacking the ability to
travel physically, the mind mentally
moves at the speed of light. Able to
rewind life back to its innocence,
it allows us the opportunity to
reminisce and reverie of beautiful
moments that could never be. It takes
us to places that we will never see
physically, because its response
to literal misery, is imaginary liberty.

"Correspondence (Part Two)"

Dear Momma,

Hello love, how is life treating you? Very well I pray, I hope to see you in a week or two. Since the last time we talked, ain't nothing changed with my predicament. My situation is still the same, and truthfully, I'm sick of it!

I'm sorry for my arrogance, I really should have listened. You tried to tell me how the life that I lived had consequences. But I didn't pay attention to your motherly intuition. When all your advice could have helped me stay out of prison.

That's water under the bridge, after all the years that I've did. I just want you to know that I love you for being here. Through all my mistakes, and through all my bad decisions. You kept me motivated with all your words of wisdom. I'll never understand how you loved me without a conscious, and stayed in my corner through all my problems and nonsense.

You told me about my phony friends, and all their contradictions, but it took for me to come to jail to truly comprehend it. So now I understand what you meant by experience, and how the game that I was playing could get me behind a fence.

Now all these years wasted for a silly reputation, when all you ever preached to me was work and education. I wish that I could explain this with a logical explanation, but all my excuses are meaningless information. It could have been avoided unless this is destiny, but I refuse to let this one mistake get the best of me.

I'll let you go for now, but know that I really love you, and there is nothing else in this world that I'll put above you. Tell the family I love them, and everything is fine with me. And I appreciate them being there in all your times of need.

Quid pro quo,
Damon Lamont Smith

P.S.
Even though I'm your child,
You are my gift!

"Ear Crack"

Chasing after Young Money in Chopper City with the product straight from Columbia, real Bad Boys keep a low Profile because they know that Black Wall Street has the Grand Hustle. Customers that Smoke-A-Lot always buy their work from the Swisha House by the G-Unit, because they are really Sic Wit It. Wanting to visit the crew of Star Tak, Tommy Boys go straight to the Bloodline with No Limit in the back room of the Suave House, while Roc-A-Fellas visit MoTown searching for Derrty Ent.. But when Cash Money starts to Get Low, Ruthless Diplomats Fresh out of the Asylum Flipmode and start working for Murder Inc… And when Warner Bros. get questioned about eh Desert Storm Aftermath, they play So So Def because they know that Jive dudes are not Bulletproof. So Ruff Riders not wanting to become State Property for Disturbing Tha Peace never Rap-A-Lot, because Poonanny that talk too Loud usually end up in D-Block on Death Row or in the Atlantic sleeping with the fishes.

"Trees"

Confidence is persecuted not for the fruit that it bears, but for the qualities that it possesses that allow it to produce those fruits. Its roots are disliked only because they are strong and deeply embedded into the Earth. While its bark is detested only because it cannot be copied by the masses, its branches are loathed only because their length and positioning are completely unique and its sprouts are hated only because they weather through every season and continue to produce. Insecurity seems to be its only rival planted among the other trees in the garden of human feelings. But under no circumstances should it be nurtured and allowed to flourish, because its flowers contain parasitical spores that will corrupt and destroy every other emotional tree that they come in contact with.

"Cognizant"

Amused by a one-sided association where the premise is to love unconditionally knowing that equal and fair exchange is not truly a part of the game. Willing to be used and abused for material and intellectual gifts and deeds consciously knowing that they will never be received. Aware that the relationship is only as important as the moment in time truly refined. For those unconscious to the stages and tools used to achieve that type of deception, fake smiles, meaningless compliments, and insincere hugs are perceived as genuine love. While those conscious to this type of behavior, silently look at elaborate attempts at manipulation as pure entertainment.

"Why"

Placed in a position where his peaceful
wishes never came to existence, his wishes
became more vicious as time made his thoughts
extremely twisted.

Revenge and retaliation became regular
thoughts in his rotation, as his situation
experienced extended durations of isolation.

Intimacy became an individual activity,
making his intimate moments exercises in
not only physical symmetry, but also in
pleasurable memory and pornographic imagery.

Separated from society his anxiety grew
quietly, until he erupted violently, mentally
and physically punishing all those that
lied to him in his times of need.

Overflowing with hatred his basic emotions
were aggravation, frustration, and agitation,
causing countless conversations to escalate
into confrontations.

Nefarious from conception his complexion
mixed with his codefendant's confession,
answers his question of "Why his life is
so depressing?"

"Illusion"

Looking at life from a different perspective, my reflection would be of a different complexion. Our ancestors would not have been taken from their birth place, mentally raped and beaten, then treated in the worst ways. Our opportunities would have included other occupations besides manual labor, the constitution would have worked in or favor, and our hue would have somewhat resembled our Savior's. Our communities would not have been flooded with narcotics, filled with alcoholics, or exposed to every other illegal product. Our families would not have had to suffer, our financial troubles would not have increased our struggles, and our seeds would have learned to legally hustle. But our reality is filled with compound tragedies, some minor injuries, but most are serious casualties. Our environments lack guidance, because our communities are polluted with drugs, gangs, and violence. Our next generation is destined to suffer our stress and strain, because their role models glorify this pain by promoting all the negative parts of the game, instead of change.

"Life's Exam"

Situations and circumstances beyond our
control, are only mathematical problems
whose solutions can be obtained by the
process of elimination.

Experience being the best teacher, true
knowledge can only be attained through
trial and error, giving our minds the
opportunity to literally process each
piece of valuable information.

Lacking the ability to change the past,
we can only learn from our past mistakes
and successes, to ensure that our future
will not contain any types of limitations.

Frequently enduring trials and tribulations,
achievements and accomplishments, unconsciously
our education continues its elevation as our existence
continually presents us with momentary equations.

"Natural"

Scared of the consequences of rebellion, many soldiers choose to watch from the safety of the sideline, instead of willingly participating in the struggle. Afraid that their contribution will be all for naught, men born to lead refuse to set the standard for those individuals born to follow. Ignorant to the ramifications of not being involved, simple indifference is usually mistaken for complete surrender, justifying all confiscations as spoils of war. While resistance becomes a victim of procrastination, lost in the abyss or personal priorities and individual opinion, where action is always a last resort. Make leaders and followers equally responsible for each other's circumstances, because those not consciously part of the solution, are unconsciously part of the problem.

"Survival"

As I watched her from a distance, her life was full of indifference. But 'Lil Momma' was vicious, on top of being persistent. Her mother was an addict, her father died from an overdose. Her brother went to prison, for murdering people over dope. She didn't have a family, nobody cared if she lived or died. But 'Lil Momma' survived through her struggles to see the other side. Her trials and tribulations were obstacles that she overcame. She learned from her mistakes, because somehow, she was immune to pain. She used her physical attributes to change her circumstances. While always scheming and plotting like a dirty fer-de-lancer. Her sugar daddies were unconscious to her ulterior motives. They all were unaware that 'Lil Momma' had no emotions. She was only the product of a blatant lack of logic. She grew up inside of the projects enduring all types of nonsense. She didn't have a conscious, her goal was self-preservation. So she used manipulation and subtle insinuations. Her victims were ignorant, because after sex they were whipped. So the never caught a glimpse of the way she straddled the fence. 'Lil' Momma" used common sense; she never hit the hands that fed her. So I watched her from a distance, while silently giving her credit.

"Smoke"

I never got the chance to say goodbye.

My other side, taken from me, was it justified?

I want to cry, every time your essence crosses my mind.

Screaming inside, every time I think of how you died.

Subconsciously, I wish that I would have apologized.

You'll never die, I promise I'm gonna keep your name alive.

One of a kind, I use your memory as motivation.

Unlike no other, I miss my brother on a daily basis.

"Thoroughfare"

Infatuated by dark days and bright nights, the streets convey information to one another through complex communication. Expressed by whispering street signs and loquacious corners, their concrete conversations vary from block to block. Avenues and Boulevards converse in foreign languages, while Courts and Drives speak in broken English passed down through their generations. And though their dialect may differ from city to county, their overall messages can be translated and comprehended into universal sentences.

"Twenty Questions"

1. Why are most Black people afraid of knowledge?
2. Why are most Black males more likely to go to jail than college?
3. Why did rock-cocaine destroy the Black community?
4. Why did jealousy ruin our unity?
5. Why are friends more dangerous than enemies?
6. Why isn't there a cure for HIV?
7. Why is hustling easier than work?
8. Why are gang members dying for turn?
9. Why are prisons warehousing instead of rehabilitating?
10. Why are parolees prone to catching new cases?
11. Why do the good die young, but the bad die old?
12. Why is it easy to get in jail, but hard to make parole?
13. Why is power so addictive?
14. Why are people with broken hearts so vindictive?
15. Why is street knowledge an illusion?
16. Why are assumptions usually incorrect conclusions?
17. Why are people judged by their pigmentation?
18. Why is the first law of nature self-preservation?
19. Why is ignorance always an excuse?
20. Why is life so abstruse?

"Palter"

Loquacious individuals that loudly boast about irrelevant accomplishments, usually draw unwanted attention.

Ignorant to the scrutiny placed upon their every move, they maneuver unconscious to their peers' dissention.

Entertaining to a certain degree, their rhetoric is tolerated through humorous condescension.

Statements whether fiction or nonfiction, reveal traces of their past, present, and future intentions.

"Her"

I tried to understand love through her.

The more I tried, the more I wanted to shoot her.

It's crazy because the more she messed up, the more I didn't want to lose her.

Family and friends told me to lose her, but between her and my sanity, I chose her.

Though my love seems to do nothing but amuse her.

Like all other bitches, she just wants to do her.

So like she uses me, I am just going to use her.

It's not her fault, but I still accuse her.

I knew the situation when she offered, and I should have refused her.

But now she's a part of me and I can't remove her.

I tried to move on, by letting another woman move in.

Hoping she would massage the places that needed soothing.

But even then, thoughts of her would cruise in.

Memories of arguments, and all the good times we had when she moved in.

She broke my heart in pieces, for trying to doubt her.

So I'm glad she left me, because life is better without her.

"Karma"

    Facing first degree murder charges, he just smiled at his arraignment. He knew that this day was coming, kept a lawyer on retainer. They set his bond at a half a mil'; he laughed at the digits. He told his lawyer to post it, so he could get out and kick it. He winked at the prosecutor as they took him out of the courtroom. Contemplating his strategy, while thinking of his next move. Only took a few hours for his paperwork to process. Then he was out of jail to set his master plan in progress. He knew he was in some trouble, so he had to handle business. He called in several favors, hoping they could find the witness. That's all that they had against him, but he knew that could convict him. He knew his moves were restricted, so he paid to get the chick hit. It only cost him a quarter slab, to get her executed. Then rocked it up for his shooter, just so he wouldn't have to do it. His problem met his solution, before she got the chance to hurt him. His alibi picture perfect, he partied while she got murdered. Called his brother at 2 am to get some information. When he told him that she didn't make it, he bought the bar to celebrate it. He left the club when it closed with a pretty broad and a bottle. But he never made it home, because he fell victim to karma.

"Time's Curse"

As the clock tick-tocks,
    seconds turn to minutes.

As the clock tick-tocks,
    minutes turn to hours.

As the clock tick-tocks,
    hours turn to days.

As the clock tick-tocks,
    days turn to weeks.

As the clock tick-tocks,
    weeks turn to months.

As the clock tick-tocks,
    months turn to years.

The clock always tick-tocks,
    because time never stops.

"Never"

I never got the chance to thank you,
    for everything that you gave me.

I never took the time,
    to appreciate how you raised me.

I never thought that you needed me,
    just as much as I needed you.

I never apologized,
    for all the nonsense that I put you through.

I never told you,
    how much I love you, and what you mean to me.

I never wanted you to be hurt,
    the day that I left the streets.

I never listened to you,
    when you knew what was best for me.

I never meant to come to jail,
    but this is just a test for me.

I never begged for your help,
    until I got in some trouble.

I never talked to you disrespectfully,
    because I love you.

I never quit hustling,
    because you taught me how to be a man.

I never asked questions,
    because you drew me a diagram.

I never changed my attitude,
    simply because it came from you.

I never seen a woman in life,
    I thought that could fill your shoes.

I never seen a mother like you,
    that always kept it real.

I never stopped loving you,
    and truthfully, I never will.

"Mistakes"

Every time I see your picture,
    it just adds to my misery.
Out of sight, out of mind,
    I pray to God you still remember me.
I want to apologize,
    for not being there when you cried.
To wipe the tears from your eyes,
    and tell you "It'll be alright."
I know your life's complicated,
    with me in this situation.
I'm sorry for being selfish,
    and causing our separation.
I was young and dumb,
    and didn't comprehend the consequences.
You were just too young,
    to understand the life that I was living.
Everything that I did wrong,
    was to make sure you would never hustle.
Every bad decision I made,
    was to make sure you would never suffer.
My life was based on a deadly game,
    I knew that I couldn't win.
I swear I would change it all,
    if I could do it all again.
I send my deepest apologies,
    and pray that you've forgiven me.
But if you haven't,
    Please learn from my mistakes, and be a better me...

        I'm sorry!

"Wildflowers"

Roses that grow in a community based on
separated unity, are nurtured from the
blood wasted over material possessions.

Their crimson red complexion is a mixture
of desperation and unsophistication,
motivated by selfish and violent intentions.

Their thorns show true resentment towards
Their environment, and are willing to
continue the useless bloodshed, because
they thirst for the vitamins and minerals
that plasma provides.

Their roots reside deep inside soil polluted
with corruption and disloyalty, making
their royalty only the plants that have
survived for generations.

Those chosen few shrubs that are immune
to the devastation, cross pollination,
and poisonous fertilization experienced
in the alleys and gangways where danger
looms, and beautiful roses bloom.

"Words of Wisdom"

A wise woman told me, "love, is sometimes worse than drugs."
She also said, "in some cases, water is thicker than blood."
She told me, "that some enemies, are better than friends."
She also said, "set my own, never follow the trends."
She told me, "that everything that glitter, probably ain't gold."
She also said, "that revenge, is a dish best served cold."
She told me, "that everything that feel good, ain't good for me."
She also said, "make the money, never let it make me."
She told me, "every dog get a day, and a good one gets two."
She also said, "don't believe rumors, because they usually ain't true."
She told me, "everything that go up, must come down."
She also said, "what goes around, comes around."
She told me, "always treat people how I want to be treated."
She also said, "never beg in vain, just when I need it."
She told me, "a horse that run fast, don't run long."
She also said, "that evil people, always reap what they sow."
She told me, "it's a very thin line, between love and hate."
She also said, "it's a big difference, between good and great."
She told me, "a bird in the hand, beats two in the bush."
She also said, "that not knowing, isn't a valid excuse."
She told me, "actions speak, louder than words."
A wise woman said, "believe what I see, not what I hear."

"Remember"

I remember every time that you told me about the world,
    and how things were very different for you as a little girl.

Every trial and tribulation that you had when you were young,
    and the racist people plotting just to keep you in the slums.

All the hardships and obstacles you had to overcome,
    and the way that people acted in the South where you were from.

How the education system wasn't set up for your needs,
    and how things changed quickly after Martin Luther King.

Why you knew the Bible thoroughly and passed it on to me,
    and why it was so important for you to learn to write and read.

How you met my grandfather, fell in love, and stayed together,
    and the reason why you made it through the bad and stormy weather.

How you raised six children, went to work, and stayed humble,
    and the strategy you used to keep your children out of trouble.

All the choices that you made, and how you learned from your mistakes,
    and why everything in life is simply based on give-and-take.

Why you taught your family principles and how to be forgiving,
    and the reason why you put all your faith into religion.

I remember each and every time you blessed me with a message,
    and I want to thank you Granny for the answers to my questions.

"Losses"

Lost my father at an early age, now I'm twenty-eight.
I think about him constantly, and I still miss him to this day.

Lost Underwood in the 80s, and I still see his reflection.
My mother cried for a week, because his death was unexpected.

Lost Tina because of jealousy, her lover was her killer.
He loved her so much he killed her, just because she hurt his feelings.

Lost Percy after a heart attack, and it hurt me in the worst way.
I'll never forget his funeral, they held it on my birthday.

Lost Kerwin outside the club, the one downtown called the "Garage".
He got shot in the parking lot, and lost his life over some broads.

Lost Tre' because he was obese, and didn't want to lose the weight.
Lost my Uncle Kenneth and my friend Reece, the same way.

Lost Ms. Hady to the cancer, she had fought for twenty years.
She stayed two doors from my Granny, the first one that gave me beer.

Lost Juan in the early 90s, everybody knows who killed him.
He got shot a couple of times, then died right outside of his building.

Lost Kurpt over revenge, and a promise to his mother.
He made good on what he said, and slayed the man that killed his brother.

Lost Ant Banks because he was at the wrong place, the wrong time.
He would have probably survived, if he had recognized the signs.

Lost Smoke G across the water, so I blame it on his friends.
He was missing for a week, before they found him in a field.

Lost Mike G Anderson, without a reason for his death.
He left his girl with two kids, so now she raises them by herself.

Lost Slick over a dice game, that turned into an altercation.
Lost Boo Man his little brother, who did the retaliating.

Lost Rocky inside his house, to what the police called an "overdoes".
He was the first person I knew, that ever died from snorting dope.

Lost Wimp in Bowling Green, he fell victim to his cancer.
He had just seen the board, and didn't even get his answer.

Lost Tamara early this year, and she didn't have to go that way.
I think about her every day, and pray she in a better place.

Lost my Grandfather to old age, and it took away my hope.
I dealt with every loss I took, but that the one that hurt the most!

"Faith"

       I send to you my deepest sympathy,
along with my purest condolences.

       I'll never feel your pain,
but I understand what you're going through.

       You've lost something that's priceless,
and nothing can replace it.

       I pray you keep the memories,
and don't lose or erase them.

       This life is filled with misery,
that has no explanation.

       But life is based on destiny,
more than on expectations.

       Everything happens for a reason,
no matter how much it hurts.

       God calls the ones he wants,
because that's how our Father works.

       There's a method to his madness,
and even though it ain't clear,

       Everyone that goes to Him,
goes somewhere better than here.

"My Life (Part Two)"

    Every soldier that I know, is either in jail or dead. In a prison that I have been to, or they stuck in the Feds. I lost my comrades over drugs, women and mail. The few that's living, I can't see them because they are stuck in a cell. Am I supposed to get upset, about the tests I failed? What I learned from doing time, each one is a lesson for real. And if I open up my heart, I know that the blessings will spill. But I heard talking too much, will get the messenger killed. That's why I keep it solo-bolo, when it comes to my peers. Because I seen it over the years, how dudes be faking in here. And the board passing out dates, for dudes that's raping the kids. But if you rob or kill something, you gonna be staying for years. Now they want me to cut my facial hair and march for a year. So I can program it out, with dudes that telling in here. Talking too much ain't been a problem in my jailing career. But I know some dudes behind the walls, that did a telling a year.

"It"

Before I had It,
    I didn't pay It no attention.
But once I knew what It was,
    I needed an intervention.
Only a little It,
    and I was instantly addicted.
After It heightened my senses,
    It turned me into a victim.
They tried to tell me It was dangerous,
    but I was ignorant.
Until It started talking to me,
    then I knew what people meant.
It called to me subconsciously,
    and changed my personality.
I couldn't understand,
    why It altered reality.
I used It in my times of need,
    to keep me calm and rational.
Then It influenced me,
    and started making me irrational.
I tried to fight Its hold on me,
    but It was stronger than I thought.
And when I thought I'd shoot It off,
    I realized It was calling shots.
It knew what I was longing for,
    and gave that to me mentally.
It took care of my wants and needs,
    and made me want to never leave.
It took me to another level,
    then It dropped me on skid row.
It took me passed my lowest point,
    that's why I had to let It go.
I thought It was my savior,
    but It was only a substitute.
It took me for a crazy ride,
    now I know just what It can do.
I'm glad I let It go,
    because It was really controlling me.
With It out of the picture,
    things are back to how they're supposed to be.

"6 Minutes"

At 11:54, there was a knock at the door. The melody was signature, so he had heard it before. Since he knew who was on the other side, he quickly handled his business. But when he finished with the locks, the door came off the hinges. The crash caught him by surprise, so he reached for his nine. A flash messed up his eyes, and he felt a pain in his side.

By 11:55, he was gagged and hog tied. And as they carried him to his stash, he caught a cramp in his thigh. The only thought on his mind, was how he got in that position? Then the answer hit him, he told them exactly to go get him.

And by 11:56, he was relieved of his bricks. Then they drug him to his safe, to take everything they could get. It was all a part of the lick, so instead of procrastinating, when they asked for the information, he gave up the combination.

So by 11:58, he just watched as they cleaned his safe. And took everything they could take, that would fit in their briefcase. His jewelry off the dresser, his pistols under the mattress. The good green in the Nike box, the keys to his Lexus. The jewelry that he was wearing, the money inside his pickets. The cds inside the case, even the movies he was watching.

He knew how robberies ended, so he prayed to himself. Because when the clock struck 12, he caught 12 to his chest. So as his soul left his body, he thought about his mistake. What took him a lifetime to get, took 6 minutes to take.

"The Crime"

His education status, was rated below average.
But his mathematics were fantastic working a package.
He managed, to learn the street's codes, principles, and policies.
While slowly accumulating money, cars, and property
His best quality, was the only reason he hustled.
To take care of his mother, and make sure they never struggled.
He sheltered his younger brother, just to keep him out of the street life.
Then moved his family, just to keep them away from street types.
It gave them a chance to see life, while he conducted his business.
And with them out of the picture, his movements were unrestricted.
He expanded his business ventures, into all types of narcotics.
And invested in major product, through a partner of his partner.
Unaware that someone was watching, nothing changed after his power move.
His routine stayed the same, the only change was how his money grew.
Everything stayed on schedule, so he started buying a dozen bricks.
Until his bubble burst, and he got a visit from the government.

"The Trial"

Before opening statements, he thought about all his charges.
And how they made him a target, before they kicked in his apartment.
They found his hidden compartment, with confidential information.
So after opening statements, they showed a tape of their surveillance.
He looked at the jurors faces, for a hint of inspiration.
But he didn't see his salvation, only disgust and irritation.
They continued his desecration, by calling all their witnesses.
One after another, until they ran through their witness list.
Phony friends and associates, undercovers and addicts.
His baby's mother, her brother and even some of his static.
Their strategy systematic, after months of preparation.
And perfect cross-examination, couldn't dispute their accusations.
They built a solid foundation, with testimony and evidence.
And ruined his defense, making his paid lawyer irrelevant.
They finished their argument, by taking time just to reiterate.
All his past mistakes, before the recess to deliberate.

"Stop"

My situation ain't no different than yours,
I see the same thing you see, walls, guards, bars, fences, and doors.
My circumstances ain't no different than yours,
I spend time inside the cell every day, thinking and pacing the floor.
My attitude ain't no different than yours,
I keep a chip on my shoulder, and always stay ready for war.
My cellmate ain't no different than yours,
we talk about the same things, money, crime, drugs, prison, and whores.
My memories of being free ain't no different than yours,
I miss my family every day, and every day I think I miss them some more.
So my wishes ain't no different than yours,
I want to go home too, so don't ask me how I'm doing no more!

"Unconditionally"

To love me,
is to tell me the whole truth.
To love me,
is to correct me when I am wrong.
To love me,
is to respect me as I respect you.
To love me,
is to understand that I am like no other.
To love me,
is to treat me the same way that I treat you.
To love me,
is to give to me the same way that I give to you.
To love me,
is to accept the good and the bad that comes with me.
To love me,
is to love me for who I am, not who you want me to be.

"Correspondence (Part Three)"

Dear Grandpa,

    I never got to tell you what you meant to me, or thank you for all the knowledge and the money that you sent to me. It really broke my heart that I didn't get the chance to say good bye. The pain was so extreme, I don't know why, but I didn't even cry. I'm sorry I missed your funeral, you know what my excuse was. I really did every crime they said I was accused of.

    But that's beside the point now, how is heaven treating you? Was you mother and father at the pearly gates to meet you? Is heaven beautiful? And by the way is it cool with you, if I write every week so we can talk the way we used to do?

    I miss the conversations with the father that I never had. When you see my dad, let him know that I ain't never mad. I know you know, it broke my momma heart the day you left the Earth. My girl ain't been the same, and she deny how much it really hurt. But "everything happens for a reason" like you used to preach. Now I understand about that thing that they call destiny.

    Now that you're an angel, momma need you more than ever now. Will you help her out and pick her up the days she feeling down? I know I need some help, but I need her more than I need myself. You feeling where I'm at? I'll trade it all to see her take a step.

    I put you on my arm, to let the world know what you mean to me. Right above my daddy, where my other father needs to be. I miss you more and more, and love you more than words could ever say. Until we meet again, I'll think about you each and every day.

                                               Quid pro quo,

                                             Damon L. Smith

P.S.
Tell the rest of
the family, if
they know it or
not they're really
missed!

"Rain Drops"

As rain drops fall from the sky, they turn
dirt into mud by showing their ability to
change the consistency of most things it
comes in contact with.

As rain drops touch the foliage, they satisfy
plants and trees by showing their ability
to nurture greenery with its motherly
components.

As rain drops connect with inanimate objects,
they produce a relaxing melody by showing
their ability to create harmony with abstract
rhythm.

As rain drops cover the Earth, they cleanse
the environment by showing their ability
to wash away physical negativity.

"Substance"

My thoughts are theoretically similar to the four basic elements that make up the physical universe.

>My fire is the zeal that motivates me to continue to live and learn from my successes and failures.
>
>My air is the ability to be creative minded and imaginative in the formation of ideas, concepts, and complex notions.
>
>My earth is the strength to remain realistic regardless of the situation, condition, or circumstance.
>
>My water is the flexibility to move with or against the grain without becoming separated from my principles and morals.

My physical being is composed of the same four elements that make up the essence of life. So physically I am a part of everything, and metaphysically everything is part of me.

"Fanciful Escape"

Though my physical situation is a combination of isolation and
solitary confinement, my mind allows me the opportunity to
evade my circumstances by creating a delusionary reality
where my fantasies have the ability to play themselves out
without any type of hindrance.

Consciously I am still enduring the miserable repercussions of
my previous shortcomings and criminal endeavors, while
unconsciously I am able to experience quixotic crusades
and imaginary adventures.

Because even though I am physically obligated to remain confined
under the conditions of my incarceration, mentally I am unrestricted
in my travels and possess the mental aptitude to transcend
the fences, walls, and military that holds my physical being stationary.

"Self-Service"

Unable to find suitable companionship for intimate encounters, individuals interested in sexual relations seek alternative means to satisfy their personal needs.

Motivated by their desire to feel orgasmic relief, their release is stimulated by manual manipulation.

Improved by the combination of memories and fantasies, individual intimacy achieves the desired reprieve.

Imagining each pleasurable moment is actually a re-creation of a past sexual demonstration. Many choose to use various forms of lubrication to enhance their self-gratification.

But when memory's imagery cannot fulfill its obligation, pornography, whether written or visual completely compensates for each individual's inability to concentrate.

"Improvise"

Unable to caress you, because of the distance between us, I instead us my imagination, to touch your most intimate places. Mentally seducing your essence without restrictions, my mind explores every inch of your composition. Slowly moving from attribute to attribute, time becomes a meaningless absolute. Seconds turn into minutes, minutes turn into hours, hours turn into days, as my thoughts run astray. Lost in the moment of my imaginary pleasure, enjoying the sight, taste, and touch of your treasure, whose value cannot be measured. Motivated with you as motivation, stimulated with you as stimulation, and satisfied by your satisfaction, my fantasies evolve from subconscious ideals into sensual actions. Compensating for the lack of genuine physicality, with vivid images created to compete with reality.

"Waves of Romance"

Her name is irrelevant, but the influence she had over my ability to love cannot be summarized inside of a description of the ups and downs that were disguised within our relationship.

While our highs were passionate adventures through paradise filled with disorganized and unpredictable showings of emotional affection and physical intimacy our lows were agonizing journeys through purgatory filled with predictable and organized showings of mental torture and verbal aggression.

Our connection though mesmerizing at times and traumatizing at others, was an educational experience that allowed me the opportunity to physically and mentally erotize, improvise, sympathize compromise, victimize, and apologize before we euthanized our commitment.

And though our existence together is no longer the situation, I still recognize my past relations with her as my introduction to love's fluctuations.

"Institutionalized"

Infatuated by illusionary characters strategically placed in positions desired by the majority, we fail to realize that their lives are not real.

Blinded by our own personal opinions and beliefs, we are easily distracted by every new and improved version of the same idea.

Unable to completely comprehend the ramifications of our actions, we unconsciously pursue the material items and lifestyles that are well out of our means.

Confident that the acquisition of said items will elevate our status within our circle or community, we rearrange our own priorities and dreams.

"Nether World"

Hades does not literally consist of fire and brimstone,
but it is filled with corrupted souls, narcotic demons,
and destructive peons. All confined in an almost
inescapable domain where every second, of every
minute, of every hour, of every day consist of literal
 punishment and torture in the realm of institutional hell,
where the walking dead are condemned to dwell
inside of an eight by ten cell.

"Trust Issues"

After years of experience dealing with the lowest of the lowlifes, I have learned a valuable lesson that calls all past, present, and future associates', partners', comrades', and friends' character Into question, because under certain types of pressure, those relationships successes give vital details that substantiate their verbal/written confessions about my criminal transgressions.

"Idiot Box (Part Two)"

Born to be Menace to Society, they acquired their Juice from playing Above the Rim. Following in the footsteps of Boyz-N-the-Hood, they hustled from Dusk til Dawn on the corners trying to get their slice of the American Pie. Tired of struggling and waiting on The Day After Tomorrow or Next Friday to get their Paycheck, they chose to make every day their Independence Day by distributing Blow to every Blues Brother and Working Girl that wanted to Light It Up. But as soon as they started to get Paid in Full, they ran into Big Trouble in Little China, because Baby Boy got Married to the Mob, and caused Four Weddings and a Funeral over four Showgirls and a Pretty Woman.

Knowing that there was going to be a serious Clash of the Titans, they called The Road Warrior, Mad Max, The Terminator, Van Helsing, and the Bad Boys, to give the Goodfellas A Long Kiss Goodnight. But after a few days of Good Will Hunting, those that didn't Die Hard became The Devil's Advocate, because they vowed to Never Die Alone and didn't want to Walk the Line.

So on Friday the 13th, all those afraid to fight like Cats & Dogs called the Kindergarten Cop, and informed him about the Murder at 1600, the shootout at the Road House, the bodies buried at the Pet Cemetery, and the distribution of White noise on Beat Street.

Fearing that the Paycheck was a part of some type of Consipracy, he informed Judge Dredd about all the Accused, and their Million Dollar Baby. But figuring that the whole Never Ending Story was Pulp Fiction, he refused to give the League of Extraordinary Gentlemen the Shaft until he was certain that they were Above the Law, because he knew that Broken Silence wasn't enough evidence to shut down the Nightmare on Elm Street.

He couldn't make them State Property because his prosecutor was Legally Blonde, and couldn't put out Sixteen Candles with Hard Rain. So even with Colors and Collateral, they all avoided The Rock, and got to continue pushing Purple Rain on Bluehill Ave, because Scarface, Blade, Doctor No, Gold Finger, Rambo, and The King of New York, lived to Die Another Day in the Belly of New Jack City.

"Synthesis"

Just because you tell a story,
doesn't always make it the truth.

There's three sides to every story,
and only one of them is true.

There's you side of the story,
that's only part of the truth.

Then there's his side of the story,
that's told from his point of view.

So if you separate the two,
it's not hard to find out what's true,

That's where you'll find the third story,
that's filled with all the truth.

"Passionate Attachment"

Our circumstances differ like day and night,
    while our commitment is the guiding light.

Trust, respect, devotion, loyalty, and admiration,
    are the puzzle pieces that make up our situation.

The curiosities and questions that deserve answers,
    will become clear as our relationship advances.

Distance is no longer an obstacle that needs to be overcome,
    it is now an opportunity for us to grow as one.

Because our dedication, discipline, and determination,
    will ensure that we reach all our aspirations.

"Real Differences"

While the ignorant choose to silently pray
tor the best outcome of every trial and
tribulation that they encounter on a daily
basis, the intelligent prepare for the
worst case scenario of every situation
they encounter while silently praying
that they don't need the preparation.

"M.A.Y.A.N.T.S. (Me and You Are Not the Same)"

My life is reality,
while your life is imaginary.

I talk it the way I walk it,
while you're just a visionary.

My thoughts are based upon clarity,
while yours are based on confusion.

I show the world the real me,
while you show the world an illusion.

What you see is what you get,
while you hide behind your façade.

I paint pictures with the truth,
while your lies paint a mirage.

And I don't care what people think,
while you're moved by people's opinions.

I was born to be a leader,
while you were born to be a minion.

"You"

I'm not impressed with your war stories and old glory,
    I have probably seen it all, so the stuff that you say is boring.

You don't have to impress me, because truthfully who am I,
    is to the point, and everything you say sounds like a lie.

Actions speak louder than words, and your movements are not depictions,
    you say this and do that, so your movements are contradictions.

I'm confused about your purpose, and curious of your motives,
    so much that I keep my comrades close, and you closer.

I never thought I'd have to watch you, but obviously I was wrong,
    because your character's in question, for making your flaws known.

Now you can tell me anything, because I don't care if it's true,
    when I have nothing else to do, I enjoy listening to you.

So if it makes you feel better stretching the truth, then do your thing,
    you have my deepest sympathy, because you believe what you're saying.

And you could probably make it right, with a good enough explanation,
    but I will never tell you, because right now you are my entertainment.

"Routine"

My every day is a mixture of the same old thing,
9 years and some change of the same old thing.
I seen dudes come and go with the same old dreams,
make parole and catch a case for the same old thing.
Come back and tell me stories about the same old schemes,
conversations full of lies about the same old thing.
Cars, clothes, drugs, whores, and the same old fiends,
every day dudes talk about the same old thing.
Everybody got a plan to get the same old cream,
so every day is de'ja' vu of the same old thing.

"The Root of All Evil"

Motivated by money and everything that it bought me,
    while ignoring all the envy and jealousy that it brought me.

Infatuated by the essence of the streets that caught me,
    while receptive to all the knowledge and wisdom that they taught me.

Naïve to the disloyalty that came with the dope game,
    while conscious of the supply and demand that came with the cocaine.

Determined to get rich so I pushed it until the cops came,
    while aware of all the risk as I bought and sold it with no shame.

Addicted to all the benefits that came with the lifestyle,
    while trying to get each and every thing that made it worthwhile.

Seduced by all the women that practiced the art to beguile,
    while chasing after hoodrats with ample bodies and cute smiles.

Conscious that nothing that I've ever done was picture perfect,
    while wondering will I always be good for nothing and worthless.

Confused about the meaning of life and what is my purpose,
    while asking myself was all the pain and hurt I caused worth it?

"Issues"

How can I love my own existence,
when I'm trapped in a dimension,
where the consequences of conscious
decisions have restrictions?

Where the fences are the cause
of my attrition, and the all
my repentance, can be broken down
into Biblical scriptures.

When my present situation motivates
my disposition, and my hatred
for the system, is my only real
commitment.

When my heart is filled with all
types of suspicions, bad thoughts
and indecisions, pure hate and
cynicism.

How can I love my own existence,
when my only real ambition is
to crush my opposition, when they
let me out of prison.

"Differently"

I would ask for your forgiveness, if I
thought that it could help me.

Trade it all, just to go back to the moment
that you left me.

Apologize a hundred times, just to keep
you in my life.

And do it all a different way, so all my
wrongs can turn to rights.

Keep every promise that I made, even the
ones I didn't mean.

Take you all over the world, and show you
things you've never seen.

Be a father to your children, and the man
out of your dreams.

Be the love of your life, and everything
that's in between.

Treat you with nothing but respect, and
slightly boost your self-esteem.

Do everything you ask of me, and treat you
like you were a queen.

I would beg for your forgiveness, if I
thought that it could help me.

Do it all over again, to change the moment
that you left me.

"Optical Illusion"

As my eyes survey the whole of her physical attributes, from head to toe she is beautiful. From follicle to cuticle, she is absolute perfection. Her complexion is the perfect mixture of coffee, cream, and butterscotch. Her skin is butter soft, without any flaws or blemishes. Her body eminent, in all the right places. Her movements flirtatious, with an obvious sense of purpose. Her clothing picture perfect, from outfit to accessories. She is visual ecstasy, and still incomplete. Because her beauty's reach is only skin deep.

"Pretty Brown Eyes"

If a picture is worth a thousand words,
    your photos were like an essay.

Your letters were like a bouquet,
    of pretty lies and clichés.

But words can't describe,
    the pain I see in your eyes.

From the pictures that you sent me,
    with the letters full of lies.

A lot of words that were meaningless,
    pages full of confusion.

Pages filled with excuses,
    and illusions of what the truth is.

It took time for me to recognize,
    and read between the lies.

Read between the lines,
    to find the place the truth really resides.

Because your smile is a façade,
    that hides the anguish underneath.

And underneath is all the pain,
    your eyes have clearly shown me.

"Correspondence (Part Four)"

Dear Father,

      How is heaven treating you? Very well I pray. I'm sad I never got to speak with you. Do you know the pain it caused me, growing up with you not around? It hurt me to my heart, that you were never there to hold me down. My momma did her best after your death to raise me by herself. She never asked for help, she only played the hand that she was dealt.

      But that's beside the point. I'm writing you so we can reconnect. So I can get the chance to know that father that I never met. I got a lot of questions for you if you got a minute. Just tell me the whole story, and start if from the beginning. Everything you remember, from you birth until your last breath. I want to hear it all, from your first until your last step.

      As far as my situation goes, they got me in the system. To suffer the consequences for some of my bad decisions. I'm truly ready to listen, so allow me to apologize. For being mad at you, each and every time my momma cried. You didn't deserve the blame, so forgive me for being mad at you. How could I be angry, when you only did what you had to do?

      With time comes understanding whose fault it was that you left me. If I knew then, the stuff I know now, things would be different. I wouldn't have to say "I'm sorry", only that I miss you.

      But know that I forgive you, and miss you more than you miss me. So much, I put you on my arm so you'll always be with me. I'll let you go for now, even though I still have a lot to say. Because now that we are on speaking terms, I'll save it for another day. Just keep an eye on me, and tell God to cut me a little slack. Until we speak again, I'll be waiting for you to write me back.

                                                             Quid pro quo,

                                                            Damon L. Smith

PS.
I never got
to thank you
for my gift.

"Concrete Jungle"

I was raised in an environment,
    where there was no retirement,
        and the only requirement
            was live for the moment.

I went to school for the diploma
    when I wasn't on the corner,
        smelling like herbal aroma,
            in the gut of the beast.

I ran the streets,
    with the dealers, fiends, and heat,
        and didn't ever go to sleep,
            because the hustle wasn't made for the lame.

I played the game,
    in the snow, sun, and rain,
        and didn't care about the fame,
            because the money was the cause of it all.

I got involved,
    with the apes, snakes, and hogs,
        and broke every decalogue,
            because the motto was to "ride 'til you die".

And I thrived,
    in the jungles of the grind,
        where the monkeys were deprived,
            and only the alpha males survived.

"Face to Face"

How can I face your face,
    when I hate your face?

And I've had reoccurring dreams,
    that I defaced your face.

I still remember how you acted,
    when I faced disgrace.

And every lie that you told me,
    while I faced my case.

So why should I face your face,
    when I negate your face?

Did everything that I could think of,
    to replace your face.

I should have never fell for you,
    but you embraced the chase.

And you were beautiful at first,
    now I debased your face.

I thought that you were something special,
    like a date with fate.

Until you left me all alone,
    after I faced the state.

"Culpable"

I used to blame you,
    for not being there in my times of need.

Until I understood,
    that I was the one that took you from me.

My actions and bad decisions,
    were what had took you from me.

And I always pointed the finger,
    instead of looking at me.

But time brought lucidity,
    now I'm only looking at me.

Because I made the bad choices,
    that took you away from me.

I chose the streets over you,
    and they took you away from me.

So I'm sorry for blaming you,
    when I should have been blaming me.

"They Love That (Part Two)"

Could it be, that I can blame my misery on the streets? Or hold a grudge against society for raising a G? Twisted the measures, that got us brothers struggling together. Suffering together, praying that these days get better. See myself trapped inside a war I know I can't win. For everyone they letting out, they sending four to the pen. Taking chances to go to prison, just to feed our children. Pulling missions and getting lifer, trying to stay out of the system. Don't blame me, just blame where I come from dirty. Because all I know is fast money, not the nine to five working. I'm a product of my environment, another statistic. To keep it realistic, I'm gonna leave out the specifics. From the streets to the system, where they got us numbered and missing. So I number my wishes, freedom come after the missions.

Who love that?

"Not Enough"

If I apologized, every time a thought of you crossed my mind, that would be at least a thousand times before the sun could set and and rise.

A thousand times, times the days of mine that I been doing time, wouldn't be enough apologies so I would put in overtime.

So over time, I'd hope that my apologies could over shine, the time and times that each and every move I made was asinine.

If I apologized, for every time I acted asinine, that would be a thousand times a thousand times a thousand times.

"Workout"

If it's true,
      what don't kill me can only me can only make me stronger.

Then I understand,
      how I can hold the world on my shoulders.

The stress and strain pounds,
      that comes with me getting older.

And the trials and tribulations,
      that use to be hard to hold up.

They're pebbles to me now,
      compared to the weight of this boulder.

So I carry them around,
      right next to the chip on my shoulder.

"Approximately"

How many times should I apologize,
      for all the pain that I caused you?

Rewind time back,
      to the time before I involved you.

Pick up the phone and call,
      for the times that I never called you.

Correct each and everything,
      that I ever did to appall you.

Take back all the trickery,
      that I used to enthrall you.

Recant all the lies,
      that I ever used when I stalled you.

Beg for your forgiveness,
      for when I verbally mauled you.

And make up for times,
      that I really should have loved you.

"Daddy's Little Girl"

Please forgive me,
    for not being there when you need me.

Believe me,
    this is not where I want you to see me.

I failed you,
    and I don't have an excuse I can tell you.

I failed me,
    but not as much as I feel like I failed you.

I didn't understand,
    that my bad decisions affected you.

But now I comprehend,
    that leaving was disrespectful to you.

Give me another chance,
    so I can repent and make full amends.

Be what I should've been,
    and do all the things that I should've did.

Make up for my mistakes,
    and right all the wrongs that concern you.

Because you mean more to me,
    than anything else in the world does!

"The Last Place"

I found love in the literal form,
    hidden in the literal norm,
        where beauty is conceived and reborn.

I found lust in the physical form,
    far from the physical norm,
        where beauty is abstract and deform.

I found pleasure in the spiritual form,
    closest to the spiritual norm,
        where beauty can comply and conform.

I found freedom in the lyrical form,
    truest to the lyrical norm,
        where beauty can be seen in a poem.

"Purgatory"

In an eight by ten cell, I found the meaning of hell.

Fire, brimstone, and all the other stuff that come with jail.

Jealousy, envy, false prophets, and atheist beliefs.

Lies, theft, murder, hatred, and homosexuality.

Crucifixions, people snitching, and numerous drug addictions.

Vicious wishes, inhibitions, and unlivable conditions.

Laxation, infestation, and ignorant conversations.

Confrontations, masturbation, impatience, and desperation.

Corruption, violent disruptions, and several levels of destruction.

Are just some of the things I noticed, in my prison introduction.

"Evolution"

Too many broken promises,
    countless crimes towards humanity.

Consequences,
    for conscious decisions and underhanded deeds.

Get back and restitution,
    for all the bullets that branded me.

Repercussions and karma,
    for all the days that I ran the streets.

Payback and retribution,
    for times I acted outlandishly.

Silent prayers and attrition,
    for years I though he had stranded me.

Repentance and atonement,
    for moments he put his hands on me.

The most important thing,
    is the happiness of my family.

And dealing with this insanity,
    really brought out the man in me.

"Contemplation"

Not a moment goes by,
    that I don't think about what could've been.

A hundred complex notions,
    about what would've been.

Another thousand ideas,
    about what should've been.

To go with the million thoughts,
    about what I could've, would've, and should've did.

"Last Walk"

Tears that no longer come from the face of a hustler, are the rain drops that fall on the gloomy days of his struggle. His emotional troubles got drowned in the drug of his choice, making his conscience's voice only a whispered echo. Trapped on death row where the best ideas are let go, his conscious mind cries while his façade shows ruthless in ruthless indifference. A million thoughts about what could've been different if only his cards changed, playing the hard game with pure talent and no experience. His longevity a minor miracle taken for granted with pure talent and no experience. His longevity a minor miracle taken for granted with each breath, he seen death in many forms and fashions while consciously ignoring the wisdom. His ways sent him to prison with the sentence of death by lethal injection, each and every appeal rejected ensuring finality. His last meal realty that every action promotes an opposite reaction, so his time subtracted from hours to his final minutes. He finally found repentance in the last place possible, inside of the feelings that were once obstacles he found belief. And within that piece of peace he found a calm that he had never know, making his dead man's walk the first steps of his journey home.

"Never Too Late"

I haven't prayed since I was young,
because of past afflictions.

And if I did,
they were only lies and contradictions.

Father forgive me for my ignorance,
and bad decisions.

Also forgive me for my crazy thoughts,
and past attritions.

Father forgive me for my attitude, a
and past commitments.

Also forgive me for the things I did,
and bad intentions.

Father forgive me for the greed I had,
and past ambitions.

Also forgive me for my habits,
and my past convictions.

Father forgive me for my feelings,
towards my opposition.

Also forgive me for my feelings,
about competition.

Father forgive me for my hatred,
and my thoughts of vengeance.

Also forgive me for the knowledge,
of the consequences.

Father forgive me for my ego trips,
and past resentments.

Also forgive me for my past sins,
and past existence.

Father forgive me for the years it took,
to find religion.

And please forgive me for the years it took,
to find repentance.

"Addict"

Unlike any other female in her pack, her addiction was completely abstract. Cars, clothes, jewelry, and all the other meaningless material that money could buy, were irrelevant in her eyes. While others found pleasure in physical consummation, she experienced her ecstasy through intimate conversations. Her drug of choice was words, beautifully put together nouns and verbs that touched her in places that hands could not. She experienced orgasms beyond explanation, trapped between the pages of romance novels that caressed her sweet spots. Attracted more to intellect than attributes, her emotional attraction to sentences and paragraphs was more than infatuation. Her admiration of proper pronunciation and punctuation, was the only love that she had ever known, lost inside the pages of her first book of poems.

"Correspondence (Part Five)"

Dear Gold Digger,

I never thought going to jail would change you. Remember our last talk, you said you'd always be the same you? That promise never came true, but it's too late to blame you. For every lie you told me, and the times you never came through. My dirty used to tell me that you were nothing but trouble, but I didn't want to listen, because I thought that I loved you.

But now I know the truth, it was only infatuation. What I mistook for love, was just simple manipulation. I used our separation to deal with all my hatred; now you're the motivation that gets me through what I'm facing.

I still think about you, and every way that you played me. Like, why'd you wait 'til I went to jail before you betrayed me? What did I do to you, to cause you to be so vindictive? I gave you everything that you wanted, prior to my conviction.

You told me that you loved me, but prison showed me realty. Your faulty personality showed me your true mentality. But that part of life, everything that's good isn't right. I'm just glad I had the sight, to see when the dark came to light.

I want to thank you for the lessons you taught me, even though I paid you. It took me all this time to realize that the streets had raised you. They made you into the woman you are, so let me apologize. I should have seen the signs, but I was mesmerized by your inner thighs.

That's my mistake, I was just under the wrong impression. I thought you loved me, when you only loved my possessions. I should have known better, you messed with me for my dividends. I thought you were my friend, now we're enemies 'til the bitter end. Until we meet again, I recommend that you comprehend, that even though I'm sorry, I'm waiting patiently to get revenge!

Quid pro quo,

B*Gee'z

P.S.
I'm gonna see you
again baby,
believe me.

"Slick Talk"

You can call me dirty names,
    and see if I care.

Because I heard it all,
    from racial slurs to colorful swears.

I been bad mouthed,
    and talked about in every way.

But I'm used to it now,
    cause it happens every day.

They talked greasy about Jesus,
    and all his brothers.

So what you say to me in one ear,
    go out the other.

People's opinions are like assholes,
    they're made to be shitty.

That's why the truth needs no support,
    because it's made to be pretty.

Grown men that start rumors,
    ain't no better than kids.

That's why I pay them no attention,
    because it is what it is.

Say the cruelest thing that comes to mind,
    and don't have mercy.

Because sticks and stones break bones,
    but your words can't hurt me.

So say whatever about me,
    it ain't gonna bother me none.

Just keep your hands to yourself,
    cause that's where problems come from.

"S.I.N.F.U.L. (since ignorant niggas fuck up life)"

Does it make me a racist,
    if I don't agree with the way my race is,

And all the bad things,
    that make up the way my race lives?

The fathers that disappear,
    and don't help our sisters raise kids,

The genes in our bodies,
    that breed envy, deceit, and hatred,

The love that we have for life,
    that makes most of us complacent,

The ignorant hopes and dreams,
    that we use for motivation,

The lack of real commitment,
    we have for our declarations,

And every other flaw,
    pointed out by the other races.

"Quid Pro Quo"

My thoughts run the gamut of what should've, would've, and could've been, if I had you in my life before my past mistakes. Before my bad breaks, before dishonesty, before disloyalty, before I knew what qualities turned me on, and before I went wrong.

But those are only wishes about an existence that I never found, so I live in the here and now where my thoughts are focused only on the present, the future, and the place that I am headed. Before you I took advantage of the things that I took for granted, but with you my take for granted has grown into understanding.

Now what could've been, can be. What would've been, will be. all because of we. **If** is no longer a part of our equation, because **when** has replaced it with a time, day, and year that our plans will turn to places.

Patience is all that we will need to live, love, and succeed, since honesty, loyalty, and respect are part of both of our creeds.

"Touch It"

While her mind and body begged for reprieve, her soul completely encouraged his touch. She had never experienced pleasure to those extremes, but her body understood the consequences of lust. Stimulated only by the feeling of his hands against her skin, her body contorted to oblige his advances. And as his finger explored every inch of her being, her mind surrendered control to her circumstances. Motivated by the pursuit of sexual intimacy, physical restrictions became only a formality. Infatuated with the thought of orgasmic satisfaction, her moral inhibitions tested her sexuality. Unconcerned with the repercussions of the moment's ecstasy, she relaxed herself at first for internal relief. And when his hands found the exact spot of her deepest ambition, her mind, body, and soul shook in unison with her external release.

"Communication"

Our trials and tribulations only helped our growing process, but we couldn't see it at first because we argued over nonsense. Our failure to communicate led to misunderstandings, plus our lack of conversation just made us take each other for granted. We confused genuine love with ulterior motives, then got angry every time we didn't get what we wanted. Our commitment was a mixture of lust and infatuation, but we couldn't see the truth through our lies and manipulation. We started with good intentions that led to our bad decisions, if only we had the wisdom we could have stopped our dissention. So instead of compromising we just agreed to disagree, and when we should have worked together we were working separately. Out attitudes were to blame because they weren't compatible, so it was either you're mad at me or somehow I was mad at you. We couldn't find understanding until we were not together, but when we broke up forever it made our friendship get better. We couldn't see it at first that we were more alike than different, but when we found out the truth it just made it easy to listen.

"Correspondence (Part Six)"

Dear Little Brother,

 What's up man, how is life playing with you? Very well I pray, I got some stuff I need to say to you. I know we don't get along, but I'm confused about the reason. Does it have anything to do with me and your cousin leaving? Are you really mad at me for the reckless way I was living? Or is it something altogether different that's causing all our friction?

 You know I'm just like your mother, and she raised me to get it done. That's why I always speak my mind, and I'm never gonna bite my tongue. I know I said some things to you you'll probably never forget. I was wrong for all my threats, that much I can admit. I didn't mean to hurt your feelings, because those were not my intentions. But I can't take back what I said, because when I said it, I meant it.

 I been gone 9 years, so put yourself in my shoes. I see life from a different angle, take a look from my view. So you can truly understand, what the system is putting me through. And see where I start messing up, so it doesn't happen to you. They tell me blood is thicker than water, but I don't think that that's true. Because I can count on one hand, the times I kicked it with you.

 I'm not trying to change your mind, I'm just seeking an explanation. So I can truly comprehend the gist of our situation. Plus I'm trying to understand what you're using for motivation. So I can somehow reopen our line of communication.

 If you only knew the truth, then you would know that I tried. And if we talk another time, I can really tell you my side. But I'm gonna let you go for now, so you can make up your mind. Until we speak again, keep your head up and eyes on the prize.

Quid pro quo,

Teddy Bear

P.S.

Always remember,

that your big brother

cares.

"Lost in Thought"

Pleasure being the destination, we moved without conversation. Silence and action without worldly distractions, enhanced the satisfaction. Intertwined in different positions unaware of physical restrictions, as we fed our addiction. Time became irrelevant, as we fulfilled every element of intimate elegance. Lust, infatuation, affection, and stimulation as we traveled from aspiration to realization. Simple memories of your essence caressing me, with a touch as pure as ecstasy, as I reverie.

"Pink Slip"

When I should be at home,
    loving her and her alone,
I'm at the strip club,
    dropping all my dollars in a tip cup.
What I don't spend on women,
    at that time getting sipped up.
Knowing when I get home,
    that it's gonna probably be a mix up.
It wasn't like that at first,
    she used to go with me and like it.
She even bought me some dances,
    just to keep our thing exciting.
But that was when we were courting,
    it all changed when we got serious.
Now she don't want to go,
    and when I ask she don't be hearing me.
I try to explain it to her,
    but she always get emotional.
And always throw in commitment,
    in her reasons why I ain't supposed to go.
Then that turns to an argument,
    that leads to ultimatums,
Between her and the club,
    like she don't know which one my favorite.
I tried to make her a deal,
    if she strip I would stay home.
But she always got an excuse,
    on just why she don't play along.
And then she want to get mad,
    when I go without her permission.
And talk to me like a child,
    because I didn't follow her wishes.
I'm not into disagreements,
    but refuse to be controlled.
So I gave her an ultimatum,
    "Leave me alone or let me go."
So she chose to leave me alone,
    and just forget about our love.
Now I'm going out with a stripper,
    that don't bitch about the club.

"Vindictive"

When I should've been faithful,
    I chose the route of infidelity.
When I should've been understanding,
    I chose to go with jealousy.
When I should've respected you,
    I chose to follow my arrogance.
When I should've put trust in you,
    I chose to make you irrelevant.
When I should've spent time with you,
    I chose to play on the avenues.
When I should've been making up,
    I chose to show you my attitude.
When I should've just let you go,
    I chose to act like I wanted you.
When I should've been acting right,
    I chose to do what I wanted to.
When I should've been listening,
    I chose to play like I heard you.
When I should've been there for you,
    I chose to watch and observe you.
When I should've cared how you felt,
    I chose to show you no sympathy.
When I should have felt how you feel,
    I chose to show you no empathy.
When I should've done more for you,
    I chose to do what I felt like.
When I should've made love to you,
    I chose to just do what felt right.
When I should've supported you,
    I chose to use and abuse you.
When I should've apologized,
    I chose to blame and accuse you.
When I should've admired you,
    I chose to leave you with mental scars.
When I should've protected you,
    I chose to make you the way you are.

"Tell Me"

How many times should I apologize,
    for all the lies that I told?
For all the mistakes that I made,
    and for all the times that I stole?
How many times should I apologize,
    for all the wrong that I've done?
For all the pain that I caused
    and for all the hurt that I brought?
How many times should I apologize,
    for all the decisions that I made?
For all the positions that I played
    and for all the suspicions that I raised?
How many times should I apologize,
    for all the laws that I broke?
For all the drugs I sold
    and all the weed that I smoked?
How many times should I apologize,
    for all the people that I shot?
For all the clowns that I robbed,
    and for all the time that I got?
How many times should I apologize,
    to have a chance to make it up?
How many times is not enough,
    and how many is way too much?

"War"

In the deepest darkest crevices of my mind, my multiple personalities engage in an ongoing battle for complete control of my physical being. Six individual entities: each with their own name, character, and affiliation, each with their own morals, standards, and beliefs, and each with their own method of dealing with every situation. Their only commonality being their struggle for power, so they engage in useless intellectual debates and frivolous arguments looking for chinks in one another's armor. But since neither one is able to gain a substantial advantage over the other, they instead choose to agree to disagree on every topic, situation, mistake, accomplishment, and experience that is endured for their analysis. Their overall strengths and weaknesses are as complex as their differences of opinion, making any type of majority compromise or resolution a lost cause or forgotten ambition.

"Currency"

For the love of dead presidents,
that love set precedence.

Over my recklessness,
in the past and the present tense.

Over communication, arguments, and conversations,
Over associations, suspicions, accusations,
Over priorities, principles, and admiration,
Over emotions, hopes, dreams, and aspirations,
Over repercussions, punishment, and consequences,
Over advice, intuition, and words of wisdom,
Over opinions, blasphemy, and he say,
Over beliefs, rumors, views, and she say,
Over jealousy, envy, and aggravation,
Over promises, honesty, and dedication,
Over affection, mutual love, and happiness,
Over commitment, sympathy, and relationships.

So for the love of dead presidents,
that love set precedence.

Over my better sense,
As long as it could get me rich.

"Excuses"

Every time I told you "I love you",
I was telling a lie.

So every time I said "I am sorry"
I didn't look in your eyes.

I don't have an explanation
of why.

And if I gave you an excuse,
it would only be a lie for a lie.

I could blame it on you,
or the times I was high.

I could even blame the streets,
or all my partners that died.

I could blame it on the hustle,
or my thirst for the grind.

I could even blame it on the world,
but it would all be a lie.

I could place the blame anywhere,
even the sky.

As long as I could justify,
a reason not to blame I.

"The Theory"

From status to statistic,
    money's exploitation runs the gamut,
        from jealousy to incarceration.

Intellect and motivation,
    only play a small part in the scheme of things,
        where opportunity and means control everything.

Goals and dreams,
    become irrelevant priorities,
        that are though about in between,
            the pursuit of seniority and evasion of authority.

Inferior minorities,
    influenced by material items and competition,
        lose control of their inhibitions,
            blinded by negative ambition.

Unaware of the consequences,
    hidden behind a beautiful façade,
        they chase a mirage,
            trying to become demigods.

"Eyes Wide Shut"

      I chose death before dishonor,
in a game without rules.
      And found out exactly,
how people can play to win and still lose.
      I've seen the trials and tribulations,
that come with living the life.
      And the power and respect,
that come with moving the white.
      I've seen how drugs can break up families,
and turn friends into foes.
      And how the money from the drugs,
can buy houses, cars, and clothes.
      I've seen the ups and downs of hustling,
that come with playing the game.
      And the jealousy and envy,
that comes with money and fame.
      I've seen how addicts lose their self-esteem,
will to live, and compassion.
      And how money can change people,
in ways I couldn't imagine.
      I've seen how drugs effect communities,
and get kids into trouble.
      And how the profit from the product,
can keep a family from struggling.
      I've seen how dealers turn into addicts,
and lose what they hustled for.
      And how a nobody can turn into a somebody,
from pushing raw.
      I've seen the pain and anguish,
that comes with being broke and disgusted.
      And the joy and happiness,
that can come from a day of hustling.
      I've seen how people can get rejected,
put down, and disrespected.
      And how people will change their attitudes
when money's in the picture.
      I've seen the ins and outs of the streets,
and why the lifestyle's so addictive.
      Until I've seen the contradictions,
between its success and consequences.

"My Life (Part Three)"

Over ten calendars have passed, since I walked through the gates. Over 3600 days, that I have given to the state. Who can I blame, for my stress and strain, heart ache and pain? If not the lame, that gave the Prosecuting Attorney my name? Or the Public Pretender, that told them I was part of a gang. That did savage things for change, and killed whoever for cain. So it ain't strange, that people telling for the fortune and fame. And got me trapped with a bunch of nuts, who just won't honor the game.

"Unbecoming"

Pick a side and sty on it,
    you can't straddle the fence.

If you do more that's in your means,
    you probably spread yourself thin.

Don't be a follower forever,
    lead and make your own business.

That's not a good look,
    it makes you seem lost and confused.

If you fake it to make it,
    you'll probably end up used and abused.

Be yourself,
    don't imitate and act like somebody else.

Because you'll never find the truth,
    if you keep using their help.

Stay away from people's shadows,
    because they darken your glow.

And stay away from indecision,
    because it hinders your growth.

If you don't know which way you're headed,
    then you will never succeed.

And that's a character defect,
    that you can pass to your seeds.

"Beautiful"

Complicated relationships and confusing associations, can find complete clarity through communication. Differences of opinion and disagreements, that cover the complete spectrum of life, can be handled without the concept of violence. Factual debates and frivolous arguments, can be resolved verbally without raising an octave. The qualities of perfection, can be broken down into a simple equation. Listening plus comprehension, equals understanding in every situation.

"Correspondence (Part Seven)"

Dear Bonnie,

What's up love, how is life treating you? Very well I pray, because I know just what the streets can do. I know just what deceit can do, and how it feels to be deceived. So I can't believe that everything you said to me was make believe. As far as my situation goes, it's filled with complications, because I'm not used to the frustrations that come with incarceration.

But that's another story. I'm trying to find out what changed you. Because after all we've been through, I figured you'd be the same you. But that "out of sight, out of mind" saying, really explains you. And it hurt my heart knowing that time apart really changed you.

So now I'm curious to know, was it love or infatuation? That caused you to have a change of heart, and break your declaration? And what is your motivation, for withholding information? And what happened to all the **me** and **you** forever conversations?

I know that there ain't no **I** in us, and that it's not all about me. But it's hard for me to comprehend how you moved on without me. Because my emotions were involved, to the point that I feel betrayed. And I can't understand, how you could up and do me that way.

Since I don't know your circumstances, that's why I'm seeking an explanation, so I can truly understand what's the cause of our separation. But I'm gonna let you go for now, so you can give it some thought. And when you write me back, just tell me why you broke my heart.

Sincerely Yours,

Clyde

P.S.
Ask yourself how
our relationship
died!

"Years Later"

I think about it more and more,
at the days go pass.

And what I could've done different,
if I was given the chance.

I put myself in this position,
chasing material things.

Unaware of the consequences,
or the problems they bring.

I can't blame nobody but myself,
for the decisions I made.

Now I have the chance to reflect,
on the position I played.

I can analyze my mistakes,
and where I messed up at.

And put my priorities in order,
so I don't come back.

I can look at life from a distance,
through the holes in the fences.

From a different perspective,
that the one I had when I entered.

"They Love That (Part Three)"

I'd trade in my life, if I could start off right. No mother working at night, no more pills and pipes. But those are dreams to me, and truthfully it needs to be. I can read between the lines, during my time confined. To understand all the crimes I did to stack my dimes. Emotions and potions, got my problems deeper than oceans. Sinking and floating, coping and hoping the pain is over. It's hard to find sanity, without no profanity. Prison it landed me dirty, for all my scandalous deeds. Routines seldom seen in the anguish it granted me. Missing my family, plotting and planning my strategy. I know that they mad at me, from living lavish to savagely. Why would I change my situation, when this is the way that is has to be?

Who love that?

"Only"

Only a call away,
if there was someone there to listen.

Only a scribe away,
if there was someone there to get it.

Only another name and number,
locked behind the fences.

Only one of the millions,
that's trapped inside the system.

Only miles from society,
but mentally it's billions.

Only a single thought,
"What if I didn't come to prison?"

"Great Oak"

It doesn't take blood,
        to show me who my family is.

I got family that not my kin,
        that loves me like I'm their kid.

I got brothers, sisters, and cousins,
        that's not related by blood.

I got uncles, aunties, and mothers,
        that show me nothing but love.

I got family outside my race,
        that loves me like I'm their own.

I got family members in jail,
        like I got family at home.

I got an extended family,
        that loves me unconditionally.

So they're the leaves and flowers,
        that make my perfect family tree.

"My Auntie"

When my mother wasn't around,
      you were mother to me.

You did everything she did,
      you were what a mother should be.

You were more than just an aunt,
      you were like a mother to me.

So your daughter and son,
      are like sister and brother to me.

You put a roof over my head,
      and treated me like your own.

You gave me food, clothes, and money,
      and let me talk on your phone.

You showed me unconditional love,
      even when I was wrong.

You came and got me from some places,
      you knew I didn't belong.

You gave me motherly support,
      along with a mother's advice.

You read me scriptures from the Bible,
      that spoke about wrong and right.

You never once turned me down,
      if I needed you day or night.

So I love you with all my heart,
      and will the rest of my life.

"Your Day"

Today is the celebration,
of the birth of an angel.

Your compassion, love, and honesty,
is truly contagious.

I thank the Lord for your presence,
I'm so glad that he made you.

And there is nothing in this world,
worth enough to replace you.

The angel holding a dove,
symbolizes your love.

Because when I feel down and out,
you're always holding me up.

You're the reason that I exist,
and I thank God for that blessing.

Your words of wisdom are the message,
and I master those lessons.

The day that God created you,
defines a beautiful day.

It was the birth of an angel,
and one of the reasons I pray.

"Interchangeable"

Your wants are my wants,
    your needs are my needs.

Your likes are my likes,
    your creed is my creed.

Your ups are my ups,
    your downs are my downs.

Your sky is my sky,
    your ground is my ground.

Your eyes are my eyes,
    your grace is my grace.

Your ears are my ears,
    your face is my face.

Your frowns are my frowns,
    your smiles are my smiles.

Your ways are my ways,
    your style is my style.

Your hurt is my hurt,
    your pain is my pain.

Your stress is my stress,
    your strain is my strain.

Your thoughts are my thoughts,
    your blood is my blood.

Your heart is my heart,
    your love is my love.

"Greatest Fear"

The only thing that I'm afraid of, is when I have thoughts of losing you. Because it took me all these years, just so I could get used to you. Our trials and tribulations, our conversations and arguments. The drive that you passed on to me, wisdom, advice, and all your strengths. The love that you have shown me, regardless of if I was wrong or right. The understanding you always had, about how I lived my life. The pride that you instilled in me, never to look for handouts. The confidence you gave me, to never be scared to stand out. Your motherly support, along with your father-like honesty, your selfless dedication, to help me out in my times of need. Your unconditional love, regardless of what the circumstance. And all the knowledge you gave me, to give me a fighting chance. The only thing that scares me, is when I have thoughts of losing you. Because you're all I've got, and that more than I need to get me through.

"My Only Regret"

My only regret,
is that I disappointed my creator.

I should've took her advice,
instead of chasing after paper.

She blessed me with life,
and all I did was throw it all away.

When I should be right by her side,
I'm in a place I can't escape.

I hope I can make amends,
for all the hurt and pain I caused her.

And pay her back for the time she gave,
to raise me with no father.

I wish I could make her proud of me,
for doing something right.

Opposed to getting in trouble,
and living the hustler's life.

My only regret,
is that I never made my mother proud.

And I pray that I get a chance,
before she dies to make her smile.

Made in the USA
Coppell, TX
29 April 2021